GIRLS GUIDES

$$ $$

Cha-Ching!

A Girl's Guide to Spending and Saving

● Laura Weeldreyer ●

the rosen publishing group's
rosen central
new york

To my mother and grandmother, for teaching me to love books.

Published in 1999 by The Rosen Publishing Group, Inc.
29 East 21st Street, New York, NY 10010

First Edition

Library of Congress Cataloging-in-Publication Data

Weeldreyer, Laura.
   $$Cha-ching!$$: a girl's guide to spending and saving / by Laura Weeldreyer. — 1st ed.   p.   cm. — (Girls' guides)
   Includes bibliographical references and index.
   Summary: Provides basic information about earning money, keeping a budget, saving and investing.
   ISBN 0-8239-2988-4
   1. Girls—Finance, Personal—Juvenile literature. 2. Teenage girls—Finance, Personal—Juvenile literature. [1. Finance, Personal.] I. Title. II. Title: Cha-ching. III. Series.
   HG179.W395   1999
   332.024'055—dc21

99-14812
CIP

Manufactured in the United States of America

Contents

bout this book

The middle school years are like a roller coaster—wild and scary but also fun and way cool. One minute you're way, way up there, and the next minute you're plunging down into the depths. Not surprisingly, sometimes you may find yourself feeling confused and lost. Not to worry though. Just like on a roller-coaster ride, at the end of all this crazy middle school stuff, you'll be laughing and screaming and talking about how awesome it all was.

Right now, however, chances are your body is changing so much that it's barely recognizable, your old friends may not share your interests anymore, and your life at school is suddenly hugely complicated. And let's not even get into the whole boy issue. It's a wonder that you can still think straight at all.

Fortunately, reader dear, help is here. This book is your road map. It's also a treasure chest filled with ideas and advice. Armed with this book and with your own inner strength (trust us, you have plenty), you can safely, confidently navigate the twists and turns of your middle school years. It will be tough going, and sometimes you'll wonder if you'll ever get through it. But you—fabulous, powerful, unique you—are up to the task. This book is just a place to start.

A Brief History of Money

Money Matters

Bread, sawbucks, dough, dead presidents, cash, scratch, bucks, greenbacks, dinero . . . Why are there so many ways to talk about money? Money provides freedom, creates choices, makes things possible. Of course, lots of great things in life are free. But money is a part of our daily lives. Understanding money—how to spend it and save it responsibly—means taking control.

Girls and women haven't always had the opportunity to earn money and decide what to do with it. Today, though, women are represented in every workplace, making important decisions about jobs and money that shape our world. It's never too early to learn about money. In fact, knowledge is even more powerful than money and opens just as many doors.

This is not a book about getting rich. You won't learn how to make a million dollars. You will learn how to make smart spending and saving decisions and how to plan financially for your future. How much money you have is not the point—most people aren't rich, and almost everyone wants more money. How you use your money and how you make that money work for you is the key.

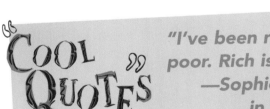

The Beginning of Money

We haven't always had money. Thousands of years ago, people used a method called bartering to get the things they needed and wanted. Bartering is a system of trading goods or services with someone for different goods or services, without exchanging any money. So a baker could trade loaves of bread with the shoemaker for new shoes. The problem is figuring out how many loaves of bread are equal in value to a pair of shoes. This became a bigger problem as people began to explore the world and travel to faraway places. How could people from two different lands trade

fairly? Both parties would have to agree on how much each good or service was worth.

In some societies, if parents wanted their daughter to marry a certain man, they had to give him valuable items such as cows or land. Sometimes the man had to give her parents such items in order to get permission to marry their daughter. This practice still goes on in some countries and cultures.

The world needed something that most people would recognize as valuable and would agree to accept in exchange for goods and services. Every society and every country developed its own "medium of exchange"—that is, things that a group of people determine to have a certain worth. Shells, beads, salt, feathers, tea, gold, and silver are a few of the objects that have served as money. As more and more people began to use money, smaller objects that were easier to carry began to be used. The first coins were made of gold and silver and were used as early as 5,000 years ago. By 400 BC, people throughout Europe were using coins.

World Currencies

In Japan it's the yen. Madagascar uses the franc. In Russia, people use the ruble. Mexico, Chile, the Philippines, and Argentina have the peso. Nigeria uses the naira, and South Africa has the rand. The United Kingdom uses the pound. At least 140 different currencies exist around the world!

Today, there are still a few places where people barter, but most of the world uses money. The United States has been using money since colonial times. People in the first colonies used money from their native countries: Spain, France, England, and Holland. Early colonists also used Native American wampum as money until the 1600s, when they began to make their own money. In 1792, after the American Revolution, the U.S. Congress created a new money system for this country, establishing the dollar as the currency unit (the kind of money that would be used).

Today all of the paper money we use in the United States is printed at the Bureau of Engraving and Printing in Washington, DC. Dollar bills are printed in large sheets, then cut apart, pressed, starched, and bundled. The bills aren't actually made of paper but from a special blend of 25 percent

In 1999 the euro became the official currency of eleven European countries: Austria, Belgium, Finland, France, Germany, Ireland, Italy, Luxembourg, the Netherlands, Portugal, and Spain. European banking and other financial transactions are now conducted entirely in euros. Euro notes and coins will be available for the public to use in 2002. These eleven countries all had their own currencies in the past but decided they would have more economic power if they shared one type of money.

cotton and 75 percent linen—it lasts longer! Our coins are made in U.S. government mints in Denver, Colorado, and Philadelphia, Pennsylvania.Our country mints about 13 billion

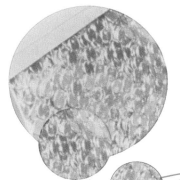

coins per year. Coins are no longer made from gold and silver. Instead they're made from copper and nickel alloys (blends), which are cheaper and more plentiful than gold and silver.

At one time or another, the United States has had a half-cent coin, a two-cent coin, a three-cent coin, and a twenty-cent coin. The largest bill ever printed in the United States was the $100,000 bill.

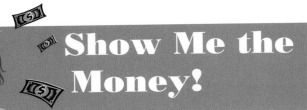

Show Me the Money!

2

Money has changed a lot throughout history, but the drive to earn money has only grown stronger—especially for pre-teens and teenagers. Money can be frustrating for teens because there are so many ways to spend it—clothes, movies, dates, cars, food—but seemingly few ways to earn it. Not true! There are numerous ways for young people to earn an income. Allowance counts as income, as does money earned from baby-sitting, raking leaves, mowing lawns, or walking dogs. Money that you receive as a birthday present can be considered income. And of course, when you are old enough, you can earn an income by getting a job at a store or restaurant. Impatient for the chance to work, some young people even start their own businesses.

Make Money at Home!

The most common way to make money is through a deal you cut with your parents, usually known as allowance. *Zillions* magazine surveyed kids around the country and found that about half of all nine- to fourteen-year-olds receive an allowance. The number goes down as kids get older, probably because other opportunities to make money come along. Most kids are asked to perform chores in exchange for their allowance.

Surveys by **Zillions** and Nickelodeon Television found that kids spend most of their allowance on fun extras like movies and CDs. Snacks come in second, and clothes and gifts rank third.

Parents like to link allowance to chores because they want their kids to learn to use money responsibly and to have a sense of pitching in to run the household. Kids don't always agree. Whatever you decide, it is best to settle on an agreement up front.

If you don't get an allowance but would like to, here are some tips for negotiating with your parents:

Plan what you're going to say in advance. Go into a talk with your parents with a well-thought-out plan. One strategy is to come up with a list of chores you will do or even a chart that will keep track of your work and the money owed to you.

 Emphasize to your parents that learning money-management skills is an important part of your life education. (This will impress them, and it's also true.)

 Assure your parents that you will act responsibly with your money. Give them examples of how you will spend your allowance.

 Remind your parents that an allowance will keep you from asking them for money all the time. (And that's the deal—no more asking for handouts.)

If your parents agree to give you an allowance, the next question will probably be, "How much?" One expert suggests one dollar for every year of the young person's age (fifteen dollars per week for a fifteen-year-old, for example). You might suggest a standard allowance that can be supplemented by occasional extras, like a clothing allowance or school supply allowance. Another possibility is to assign a price to each chore and then be paid for whatever you do. (For example, making your bed all week might be worth five dollars, washing the dishes, two dollars, and so on.) Try to be reasonable about what you ask for. You're more likely to get your parents to agree if you ask for ten dollars a week rather than fifty.

It is most important that you and your parents decide in advance how your allowance will work. In order to keep a hassle-free household, you'll want to discuss the following questions:

What do I have to do to earn my allowance? *List all chores. Decide whether you will be paid per chore or whether you have to complete all chores to get paid. Also, establish a deadline. (For example: All chores must be completed by Friday at 5 PM.)*

When do I get paid, and by whom? *Both you and your parents need to know the day on which allowance is paid so that you can budget accordingly.*

How do I get paid? Will I receive the total in cash? *Do you want your parents to put a portion of your allowance into a savings account for you? One teen worked out a banking system with her parents: They deposited her allowance into an account each week. She kept track of her total in a notebook. When she needed money, she would make a withdrawal from her account. The advantage to this system was that she had to think about and plan her purchases instead of buying something as soon as she saw it. This may sound like a pain, but it is a smart money management strategy.*

How will we keep track of work done and money owed? *A notebook or a chart on the fridge can be useful.*

What is the best way to remind my parents that I am owed allowance? *(Hint: Yelling at them is not the correct answer.) Parents will forget because—believe it or not—they're human. Find a nice way to remind them.*

Your parents have the right to expect that you will pitch in around the house without getting paid. After all, your parents provide a lot for you—food, a home, support, love, those kinds of things. Being part of a family carries certain responsibilities. Some families make two lists of chores. One lists those that you are expected to do because you are a contributing member of the household. The other list is of chores that will earn an allowance. Some families even have a third list: for every chore completed, a certain amount is deposited into a college savings fund.

Beyond Allowance

Not everyone has parents who work or who can afford to pay an allowance. Raising a family can be very expensive and sometimes allowances cannot take priority in the family budget. This can be very tough, but there are other ways enterprising young people can earn money.

You may think that it would be great to get a regular part-time job. Those jobs, however, are not available in most states until you are fifteen or, more commonly, sixteen years old. Until then, you might consider being your own boss. Young people start successful businesses all the time. You can start a baby-sitting service, a lawn-mowing business, a pet-watching business, or even the classic lemonade stand. There are lots of Web sites that give advice on how to start your own business, including ideas from other young people. Check out the resources listed at the end of this book for inspiration.

Now That's Inventive!

When K-K Gregory was ten years old, she noticed that her wrists got cold and wet when she played outside, even if she had mittens on. Instead of complaining, she invented Wristies®, fleece wrist coverings that are worn alone or under gloves and coats. K-K patented her idea and started her own company to sell Wristies, which have become a huge success.

Learning and Earning

Pssssst—want to make lots of money? Here's a secret: The more school you complete, the more money you are likely to earn in your lifetime. The more years of school under your belt, the better your chances of remaining employed and qualifying for a job that pays well. Someone with a college degree will earn more than someone with only a high school diploma—and far more than a high school dropout. Getting an advanced degree (a master's or doctoral degree) boosts your earning power even more. Check out these statistics from the United States Census Bureau:

Average lifetime earnings of:

A high school dropout	$ 609,000
A high school graduate	$ 821,000
An associate's (two-year) degree holder	$ 1,062,000
A bachelor's (four-year) degree holder	$ 1,421,000
A master's degree holder	$ 1,619,000
A doctoral degree holder	$ 2,142,000
A professional (law, medical, etc.) degree holder	$ 3,013,000

The numbers speak for themselves!

More than Money

If making money is less important to you than making the world a better place, you're not alone. A survey of U.S. middle schoolers found that most would be willing to give some of their allowance money to charities to help feed hungry children in poor countries.

Let's Spend!

3

Learning how to spend your money responsibly is just as important as learning how to save. Young people are an increasingly influential group of consumers. In 1997, kids between the ages of four and twelve influenced more than $180 billion in purchases. And today more advertising is targeted at teens than ever before.

According to **USA Today**, kids ages eight through seventeen average slightly more than a dozen shopping trips per month and average about $25 per trip. Girls spend an average of $25.58, whereas boys shell out an average of $24.44.

Are you a big spender? Does money burn a hole in your pocket? Or is saving second nature to you? Do people refer to you as a miser, tightwad, or penny-pincher? It is certainly best not to go to either extreme, but spending and saving each has its place. When you have money, you have to make a choice about what to do with it: how much to save and how much to spend. You make choices about what you need (like food or a warm coat) and what you want (like going to the movies or a new computer game), while also remembering your responsibilities (like buying a birthday present for your grandmother or making a donation to charity).

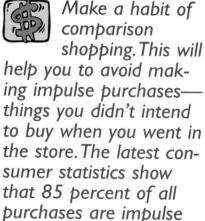

Tips for Healthy Spending

Make it harder to gain access to your money—try putting your money in a bank account or leaving your cash or ATM card at home.

Make a habit of comparison shopping. This will help you to avoid making impulse purchases— things you didn't intend to buy when you went in the store. The latest consumer statistics show that 85 percent of all purchases are impulse

buys. Distinguishing between needs and wants will help you to avoid impulse buying. Ask yourself, "Do I really need this, or do I just want it?"

 Avoid shopping when you are hungry, tired, rushed, or depressed—you're more likely to make unwise, hasty choices.

 Set a goal to purchase something you really want and save your money to buy it. Having a specific goal will give you the incentive you need to save money.

 One expert suggests taking a calendar and marking off special dates that you need to remember, such as birthdays, Valentine's Day, Christmas, and vacations. Planning ahead helps to eliminate unexpected expenses.

Be an informed consumer. Companies that make everything from candy to skateboards regularly pay big bucks to experts in psychology and marketing to learn how to capture you and your friends as customers. The last thing companies want is for you to be too well informed, because the more you know, the less easily you will part with your spending money. Think about what you're buying and why you are buying it!

If no other strategy works for you, stay away from stores altogether.

Budget Is Not a Dirty Word!

The easiest way to make sure that you have enough money for the things you want is to make a budget. A budget is a plan for how to spend your money.

When you make a budget, you should first list your income—money coming in from a job or your allowance. Add up all of your income.

Next list your expenses—all the ways your money goes out. First list your fixed expenses. Those are what you are spending money on every month, and they basically stay the same from month to month. Are you paying for a health club membership? Your Internet service provider? A pager or cellular phone? What about transportation costs—how much do

My Budget

INCOME ....$

EXPENSES

health club membership ...$

Internet provider ....$

bus ....$

cell phone ....$

pager ....$

food ....$

movies ....$

clothes ....$

CDs ....$

TOTAL: $

INCOME: $

TOTAL: —$ _____ = SAVINGS

you spend on bus or subway fare to school? All of these go on the list. Then think about everything else you spend money on during the month. Snacks, movies, and other incidentals can really add up. You may need to estimate in some cases, but it will be easier (and more realistic) if you keep receipts from all the purchases you make in a standard week.

Don't forget to take into consideration anything that you are saving for. If you want to buy a new bike and you are saving five dollars per week toward the price of the bike, put that in your budget to make sure it happens.

Now add it all up.

You should have two figures. If your income is more than your expenses, congratulate yourself. If the two numbers, incoming and outgoing, are equal, then you have a balanced budget. If you're like most people, though, you have more going out than you do coming in. So what do you do now?

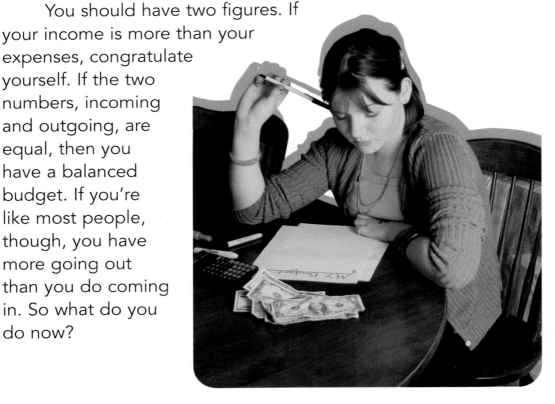

"I have enough money to last me the rest of my life, unless I buy something."—Anonymous

The next step is to take a good hard look at the expense items you listed. You are going to make two lists of expenses—wants and needs. It is important to remember that this is your budget, and nobody can tell you how to make it. That's part of the fun.

Your "needs" list should include any regular fixed bills you have such as transportation, school-related expenses (lunch, field trips, club dues, and so on), and essential clothing. Needs are non-negotiable—you can't cut them out or pay less for them—and they have to remain a part of your budget. Your "wants" list will include more fun stuff, and it will be flexible. If you have to trim your

budget, items on the "wants" list are the first to go. You have to set aside money to take the bus to your after-school job (a need), but you may not be able to buy the new pair of shoes you've been eyeing at the mall (a want). Don't cut out all of your wants unless you have to, though. The idea is to make a budget you can live with. It can get depressing looking at those cold hard numbers.

It may seem as if there are unlimited places for your money to go. Budgeting means gaining control. Balancing your budget means figuring out where you can cut costs to save money. Find out where to buy things at bargain prices. (Ask friends or consult the library for tips.) Check out your local used CD and book stores. Almost every town has at least one, and larger cities have lots. A used CD costs only half as much as a new one, and the music doesn't sound any different.

Think about buying clothes at thrift stores, consignment shops, or discount stores. You can find good deals— and great new looks—if you hunt for them.

Don't let the budgeting process get you down. It may seem as though you'll never have enough money for all the things you want and that you'll have to look on in envy while your friends go on shopping sprees. But chances are pretty good that nothing like that will happen. Get a handle on your finances now, and you can make sure that it never will.

A Challenge (If You're Up for It)

If you are not currently responsible for buying your own clothes, you might ask your parents if you can be, as a way of learning to manage money. You could suggest that you receive a monthly clothing allowance or that you receive a larger sum twice a year, once before school starts and once in the spring. You might need to ask your parents for help on what to buy and when, but this is a great way to improve your budgeting skills. You'll also get some real-life experience in making choices: "I want those jeans, but if I buy them, I won't have enough to get new shoes for school. What's more important? What is my priority? What do I need, and what do I want?"

Money Doesn't Grow on Trees
(But It Can Grow)

5

Now that your budget is complete and you have some sense of what you spend money on, is there anything you want to do or need to buy that you can't afford? Do you have any goals for your money? Most people do.

There are short-term goals and long-term goals. Here is an example of a short-term goal: "I want to buy a new outfit for the school dance. It's going to cost over $100, and I don't have enough money. I need to save my money in order to accomplish my goal." A long-term goal takes much longer to accomplish: "I am in seventh grade, and I already know I want to go to college when I graduate from high school. I need to start saving my money now so that I can afford to go to college."

Both of these goals require planning and saving. What are your short-term and long-term goals? You may want to buy some new makeup next week, and you might plan to own a cosmetics company in ten years. How can you reach each of these goals? The answer to this question depends on you and your spending habits. You are the only one who knows what it will take to make you save.

Once you have made the decision to save, you might consider putting your money in the bank. Opening a savings account is a good way to start saving money.

The first thing you need to do to start a savings account is to pick a bank. The bank you pick will usually depend on two things: the bank's location and the interest rate it offers. Interest is a percentage of your total savings. The bank pays you interest in exchange for allowing your money to stay in it. You will want to find the highest interest rate. The higher your interest rate, the more money will be added to your savings account. You should also be certain that the bank is insured by the Federal Deposit Insurance Corporation (FDIC), a government-run company that insures the deposits in banks. Even if an FDIC-insured bank goes out of business, the money in it

will still be protected. Almost all of the banks in the United States are insured by the FDIC.

Next go into the bank, and tell someone who works there that you want to open a savings account. He or she will ask you to fill out a form with your name, social security number, and address. Your parents will be asked to sign the form if you are under eighteen. You will also be asked for identification, such as a birth certificate. After you complete the form, you will need to deposit some money to start your account; this is called a minimum deposit. The usual minimum deposit is at least fifty dollars, but it varies from bank to bank.

Stat Chat

According to Teenage Research Unlimited, about 66 percent of American kids between the ages of twelve and fifteen have a savings account.

There are different kinds of accounts in which you can save money. Your choice will depend on your goals for your money. Weigh the benefits of each.

Statement savings account:

This is the most common kind of account. Every month you will receive a statement from the bank that shows your withdrawals and deposits, how much interest you have earned, and how much you have in your account.

Passbook savings account:

This account is very similar to a statement savings account, and it usually pays the same interest rate. Instead of getting a statement in the mail, however, you have a passbook. Each time you make a withdrawal or deposit, the bank teller records it in your passbook along with any interest earnings and your total account balance.

Checking account:

Most people have both a checking and a savings account. Checking accounts hold your money just as savings accounts do, but usually you don't earn any interest on the money. Instead you will be able to write checks by drawing on the money in the account. Checks allow you to pay for things without carrying cash. Most banks require you to be eighteen years old to open a checking account, though some will let you open one if a parent or guardian puts his or her name on the account in addition to yours.

Certificate of deposit (CD):

If you have some money that you don't plan to use for a while, you can put it into a CD—not a compact disc, but a certificate of deposit. With a CD, you agree to leave your money in the bank for a specified amount of time, like six months or a year. Since the bank knows how long it will have your money, it will pay you a higher interest rate than you would earn with a regular savings account. The catch? If for some reason you need the money before the time is up, you will have to pay a penalty—a fee for withdrawing the money early. You usually need at least $500 to start a CD.

Money market account:

This account will pay more than a regular savings account (but a little less than a CD) and let you withdraw money by writing checks. It's a very good deal, but there are some limitations. Generally you can make only a certain number of withdrawals each month, and you have to maintain a large minimum balance in the account—usually $1,000 or more.

Individual Retirement Account (IRA):

An IRA is a savings account for retirement. This may seem like long, LONG-term

planning, but if you're patient, it's a great deal. When you put a percentage of your income into an IRA, you don't have to pay any taxes on it until you take it out of the account. Once you are retired and take the money out, you will pay less in taxes. It's like a reward for saving.

Understandably, you may be thinking that it is pretty silly to save now for something that is probably at least fifty years away. Actually it's simple math: The younger you are, the greater advantage you have, because time is on your side. Teenagers have the greatest number of years ahead of them to make their savings grow. If you start an IRA with just $50 and earn 10 percent interest a year, you'll make only $5 in your first year. But the next year, you will earn $5.50. Even if you don't add another penny to the account, you will still have more than $100 after ten years. Most people do add to their IRA every year, though, and the money grows quickly. By the time you have $10,000 in your account, that same 10 percent will be $1,000.

1st yr. $50--10%=$5.00

2nd yr. $55--10%=$5.50

Take the Credit

Should someone your age have a credit card? Credit cards seem so easy, don't they? They allow you to buy things without any money, so purchases seem as if they are free. But they're not. Credit means that a bank or business is willing to lend you money and give you some time to pay it back. The catch? The banks charge you interest—a lot of interest—on the money until it is repaid.

The laws are different in each state, but most states require that you be eighteen or twenty-one in order to receive a credit card. You may think that this is unfair, but banks do not want to lend money to someone unless they feel confident that the person can repay the loan.

Credit cards make it very easy to get into debt. Without planning or saving or even thinking twice, you can buy to your heart's desire. Lots of people get into trouble with credit cards, running up huge debts that get bigger—and harder to pay—because of interest charges. When you are old enough and think you are ready for a credit card, consider a few pointers:

Choose your card carefully, and limit yourself to one.

Read and make sure that you understand your credit agreement. If you have any questions, ask a parent for help or call the credit company. Some cards make you pay an annual fee just to use them. Find out in advance all the fees you will have to pay.

As with everything else, you should always comparison shop for the best deal. Look for the credit card that offers the lowest interest rates to save yourself money.

 Don't charge everything you buy. Pay cash whenever possible. It is always cheaper to pay cash.

 Continue to plan your purchases carefully. Credit cards are not free money or a license to spend.

 Be very careful when using your credit card over the phone or over the Internet. Your credit card number can be stolen and used to make purchases. If your card is stolen or you think your number is being used illegally, call the credit card company immediately and report it. It will cancel your account and issue you a new card. If someone uses your card to buy things, under federal law you may be responsible for paying the first $50 charged to your card.

Investing

Investing may sound dull. It may make you think of stuffy people in boring business suits. But investing can be a great way to make money, and it's not too early to start learning how to do it. Just remember that investing means taking a greater risk of losing money than you would have with an ordinary savings account.

How you choose to invest your money has to do with how much risk you are comfortable taking. You have to decide which kind of investment suits your needs. The main types of investments to consider are stocks, bonds, and mutual funds.

"The only way not to think about money is to have a great deal of it."
—Edith Wharton,
The House of Mirth

Stocking Up on Stocks

A stock is a share, or piece, of a company. When you

own a share, you own a very small part of a business. Buying stock means making an investment in a company. Imagine that each share of stock is one brick in a building; if you own a brick, you own a piece of the building. When decisions are made about how to use the building, each brick represents one vote in the decision-making process. The more bricks you own, the more power you have to influence decisions.

When a company needs to raise money, it may choose to sell part of itself to the public. Coca-Cola is an example of a publicly traded corporation, and millions of people own a piece of the company. Publicly traded businesses sell stock to anyone who wants to buy it. Companies that are publicly traded are listed on stock exchanges, places where stocks are bought and sold. To buy stock in those companies, you have to use the services of a stockbroker.

People buy stock in order to make money. If you buy stock, you are betting that the business will do well and make a profit. When the business does well, the value of its stock goes up. The flip side is that if a company does poorly, you can lose money as its stock goes down in value.

Investing in stocks can be tricky. Companies have bad times and good times. As a part-owner of the company, you can decide how long to hold on to your shares and when to sell them. Along the way you may receive dividends, which are profits divided up among all stockholders. Dividends may be paid in the form of money or as additional shares of stock.

Let's imagine that you bought fifteen shares of Reebok stock for $20 each. Your initial investment would be $300. Two years later, Reebok has had extraordinary sales and is hugely successful. Now Reebok stock sells for $47 per share, so your fifteen shares are worth $705. If you decide to sell now, your profit will be $405. Next imagine that the following year, Nike's new shoes are the big thing, and Reebok's sales go way down. Suddenly each share of stock is worth only $15—$5 less than you originally paid for each share—and you have lost money. You will have to decide whether to sell now or hold on to your stock, hoping that the stock will rise in value again.

You probably didn't win the first time you played Monopoly. Do you want to gamble with real money the first time you enter the stock market? You don't have to invest real money to get experience: You can set up a practice portfolio and pretend to divide your money among a number of stocks or other investments and follow their status. America Online and many other Internet providers will allow you to set up a practice portfolio on-line and receive daily updates about your "stocks" via e-mail.

Whether you decide to start with a pretend portfolio or a real one, you need to answer some questions: How long will it be before you need your money? How much are you willing to risk losing? Many advisers say that you should plan to keep most investments for five to ten years, which seems like a lifetime when you're fourteen. The sooner you're going to need your money, the less risk you should take.

If you decide to invest for real, as a minor you will need a parent or guardian to open your account. Look for a broker who is well recommended by someone you trust. If you're lucky, you will find a broker who wants to encourage young people and will take on a teenager with a small account. You might even find a broker who will charge you low commissions. Commissions are the fees brokers charge for buying or selling stocks, and they can eat up profit for a small investor.

A stock that is not listed on a major stock exchange (such as the New York Stock Exchange or the Tokyo Stock Exchange) and sells for less than $5 per share is called a penny stock.

Buying Bonds

Bonds are another type of investment. Buying bonds is like lending money to a company instead of buying a piece of the company. When you buy a bond, the seller promises to pay you back with interest after a period of time—usually ten years or more. Bonds are generally a safe investment as long as the seller of the bond is trustworthy. Local, state, and federal governments also sell bonds, and government bonds are generally the safest choice. Corporate bonds often pay higher interest rates than government bonds, but they can be riskier because the companies that issue them may not be able to pay you when the bond is due.

Bonds usually pay higher interest rates than short-term investments like stocks, but you have to be willing to wait a long time to get your money back. Many investors choose a mix of stocks and bonds so that they have both short-term and long-term investments.

The Fund Is Mutual

Another choice is to put your money into a mutual fund. "No-load" funds do not involve any commissions, and you can often start with an investment as small as $250. The business section of your library or bookstore will carry directories of mutual funds. Typically these directories describe a fund's performance (how much money it has earned or lost per year) and the types of companies it invests in, as well as providing phone numbers for more information. Knowing which companies a mutual fund invests in can help you decide whether or not to choose that fund. If you love Macintosh computers, for instance, and you find a mutual fund that invests in Apple, it might be the right fund for you.

Mutual funds can be low or high risk. With a variety of investments, mutual funds do not depend on the success of any one company. A mutual fund that invests in bonds and blue-chip stocks (valuable stocks that are unlikely to lose their value) is a safe, stable type of investment. A mutual fund that invests in small companies or technology is much riskier.

Do your research before you make any choices about investing. Your broker will help you, or you can call the companies for information and follow their stock prices in the newspaper or on-line. Remember, however, that there is no way to predict the future performance of any stock or mutual fund, even if it has performed very well in the past. That is why you're better off starting with a few practice investments.

Be Money-Wise

Money is not the most powerful force in the world. Many things in life—love, friendship, happiness—have value that can't be measured in dollars. Still, money is a fact of everyday life. You can't avoid making choices about money: how to earn it, how to spend it, how to save it. So instead of being afraid or reluctant to deal with money, be confident about your knowledge and take control. If you make mistakes, learn from them and try again.

In the past, women were seen as too silly or flighty to handle money (even though most of them managed the finances for their household, which is hard work). Today women hold important positions in large companies and make major decisions about money every day. With the tools you have now, you'll be able to join them in a few years.

This book has been an introduction to money concepts that you will encounter and use for the rest of your life. No one book can teach you all that you need to know about money, but you are well on your way to learning one of life's most important lessons: how to rely on your own power to make smart decisions.

bartering Trading or exchanging goods or services for other goods or services.

bond A type of investment. When you buy a bond, you are lending money to the seller; the seller will pay you back with interest after a specified period of time.

budget A plan for keeping track of your income and expenses.

certificate of deposit (CD) A type of bank account that pays interest on money deposited and kept in the account for a specified period of time.

checking account A type of bank account that allows you to write checks for the money in the account.

currency Coins, bills, or any object used for purchases and other money transactions.

individual retirement account (IRA) A long-term savings account that earns interest. The money must be left in the account until retirement to collect the full interest.

interest A payment added to an amount of money that is a percentage of the amount.

investment Money that is put away or used for the purpose of earning additional money through interest and other gains.

mutual fund A company that invests money in stocks and bonds sold by other companies.

portfolio An individual's collective stocks, bonds, and other investments.

savings account A type of bank account that pays interest on the money in the account.

shares Portions of ownership of a company.

stock The ownership or partial ownership of a company.

stockbroker A professional who manages the buying and selling of investments for individual investors.

stock exchange A market for the buying and selling of stocks.

Money Resources

The Jump$tart Coalition for Personal Financial Literacy
919 18th Street NW, Suite 300
Washington, DC 20006
Phone: (888) 45-EDUCATE [338-2283]
Fax: (202) 223-0321
e-mail: info@jumpstartcoalition.org
Web site: http://www.jumpstartcoalition.org
Publishes books and other materials that teach young people about managing money.

National Center for Financial Education
P.O. Box 34070
San Diego, CA 92163-4070
(619) 232-8811
Web site: http://www.ncfe.org
Publishes a catalog that includes allowance "kits" as well as books for kids and parents.

Zillions
P.O. Box 54861
Boulder, CO 80322-4861
(800) 234-2078
Zillions magazine is a good source of information on how to manage money and spend wisely. Published by Consumers Union (the publisher of *Consumer Reports*), it comes out six times a year.

Web Sites

Cash University
http://www.cashuniversity.com/

Department of the Treasury's Kids' Page
http://www.ustreas.gov/kids/

Investing for Kids
http://tqd.advanced.org/3096/

Kids Consumer Corner
http://tqjunior.advanced.org/3643/

Kids' Money
http://pages.prodigy.com/kidsmoney/index.htm

Money Cents: Making Money Make Sense for Kids
http://www.kidsmoneycents.com

on2: Money
http://www.pbs.org/newshour/on2/money.html/

Teen Guide to Making Money
http://www.fileshop.com/personal/gbyron/page1.html

The Young Investor
http://www.younginvestor.com/pick.shtml

Erlbach, Arlene. *The Kids' Business Book.* Minneapolis, MN: Lerner Publications Company, 1998.

Godfrey, Neale S. *Neale S. Godfrey's Ultimate Kids' Money Book.* New York: Simon & Schuster, 1998.

Jeffrey, Laura S. *Great American Businesswomen.* Springfield, NJ: Enslow Publishers, Inc., 1996.

Karnes, Frances A., and Suzanne M. Bean. *Girls & Young Women Entrepreneurs: True Stories about Starting & Running a Business Plus How You Can Do It Yourself.* Minneapolis, MN: Free Spirit Publishing, Inc., 1997.

Kravetz, Stacey. *Girl Boss: Running the Show Like the Big Chicks.* Los Angeles: Girl Press, Inc., 1998.

McQuinn, Conn. *Kidbiz: Everything You Need to Start Your Own Business.* New York: Puffin Books, 1999.

Nathan, Amy. *The Kids Allowance Book.* New York: Walker Publishing Co., 1998.

Otfinoski, Steven. *The Kid's Guide to Money: Earning It, Spending It, Growing It, Sharing It.* New York: Scholastic, 1996.

Resnick, Abraham. *Money.* San Diego, CA: Lucent Books, 1995.

Roper, Ingrid. *Moneymakers: Good Cents for Girls.* Middleton, WI: Pleasant Company Publications, 1998.

Young, Robert. *Money.* Minneapolis, MN: Carolrhoda Books, 1997.

Index

About the Author

Laura Weeldreyer works on public school reform at a nonprofit organization in Baltimore, Maryland. A former teacher, she is also the author of *Body Blues: Weight and Depression*. Ms. Weeldreyer devotes her time and energy to issues that affect young people.

Acknowledgments

Many thanks to Doug Fireside, class 8-70 at Robert Poole Middle School, Michele Drohan, Erika and Lisa, my friends, and my family for the richness of your advice and support. Special thanks to my brother, John, for being our family financial guru.

Photo Credits

Cover photo by Thaddeus Harden; p. 5 © Harry Bartlett 1998/FPG; p. 7 © CORBIS; p. 9 © Archive Photos; p. 10 © Ron Chapple 1998/FPG; pp. 10, 11 © Bureau of Engraving and Printing, Washington D.C.; p. 11 courtesy of the American Numismatic Association; pp. 12, 14, 15, 16, 17, 21, 24, 26, 29, 35, and 41 by Thaddeus Harden; p. 18 courtesy of Wristies®, Inc.; p. 37 © Bernard Gotfry/Archive Photos; p. 38 © Telegraph Color Library 1990 /FPG; p. 42 © Patti McConville/Image Bank.

Design and Layout

Laura Murawski